For my beloved Charlotte, a most clever six-year-old girl
who delights in anything ridiculous
—J. A. S.

For my Arden, a young lady of wit, whimsy, and wisdom
—V. S.

BLOOMSBURY CHILDREN'S BOOKS
Bloomsbury Publishing Inc., part of Bloomsbury Publishing Plc
1385 Broadway, New York, NY 10018

BLOOMSBURY, BLOOMSBURY CHILDREN'S BOOKS, and the Diana logo
are trademarks of Bloomsbury Publishing Plc

First published in the United States of America in March 2021
by Bloomsbury Children's Books

Bloomsbury books may be purchased for business or promotional use.
For information on bulk purchases please contact Macmillan Corporate and
Premium Sales Department at specialmarkets@macmillan.com

Library of Congress Cataloging-in-Publication Data
Names: Stirling, Jasmine A., author. | Stamper, Vesper, illustrator.
Title: A most clever girl : how Jane Austen discovered her voice / by Jasmine A. Stirling ; illustrated by Vesper Stamper.
Description: New York : Bloomsbury, 2021.
Summary: *A Most Clever Girl* follows Jane Austen's journey to hone her craft,
finding her place in the world amid joys and sorrows and writing her famous novels.
Identifiers: LCCN 2020028130
ISBN 978-1-5476-0110-3 (hardcover) • ISBN 978-1-5476-0111-0 (e-book) • ISBN 978-1-5476-0112-7 (e-PDF)
Subjects: LCSH: Austen, Jane, 1775–1817—Juvenile literature. | Novelists, English—19th century—Biography—Juvenile literature.
Classification: LCC PR4036.S75 2021 | DDC 823/.7 [B]—dc23
LC record available at https://lccn.loc.gov/2020028130

Book design by Jeanette Levy
Printed in China by Leo Paper Products, Heshan, Guangdong
2 4 6 8 10 9 7 5 3 1

All papers used by Bloomsbury Publishing Plc are natural, recyclable products
made from wood grown in well-managed forests. The manufacturing processes
conform to the environmental regulations of the country of origin.

To find out more about our authors and books visit
www.bloomsbury.com and sign up for our newsletters.

A Most CLEVER Girl

How Jane Austen Discovered Her Voice

Jasmine A. Stirling

illustrated by Vesper Stamper

BLOOMSBURY
CHILDREN'S BOOKS

NEW YORK LONDON OXFORD NEW DELHI SYDNEY

Jane loved stories—long ones, short ones, worn and new.

But there were some kinds of stories that she just couldn't stand.

These were pale stories with delicate ladies who fainted all the time. (ALAS!)

Or gloomy stories with orphans on doorsteps and terrible secrets in the attic. (OOOH!)

Or sticky-sweet stories where people fell in love at first sight. (EWW!)

This was the fluff that was fashionable in those days.
Jane found it, well, stale. And predictable.

You see, Jane *had a lively, playful disposition,*
which delighted in anything ridiculous.

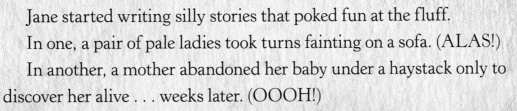

Jane started writing silly stories that poked fun at the fluff.

In one, a pair of pale ladies took turns fainting on a sofa. (ALAS!)

In another, a mother abandoned her baby under a haystack only to discover her alive . . . weeks later. (OOOH!)

In yet another, two children were so hungry they bit off their mother's fingers. (EWW!)

She read the stories to her family, and they couldn't stop laughing.

Jane's family lived in a rambling house in the English countryside, surrounded by fields, flower gardens, and strawberry beds. The house, called Steventon Rectory, overflowed with people: Jane's parents, their six sons and two daughters, a couple of servants, and, for much of the year, three or four boys who lived with them and were educated by Jane's father.

Words echoed joyfully through the house. Her mother wrote and recited poetry in one room while her brothers debated the news in the next. Jane and her sister, Cassandra, sang songs upstairs as her father taught the wonders of Shakespeare to students below.

On magical days, Jane's whole family staged plays in their barn. Together they designed the sets, sewed the costumes, and performed all the roles.

Words made Jane happy. Her family made her happy. Jane *knew her own happiness* and chased it.

Except . . . with all this happy noise in
the background, Jane couldn't find a quiet
place to write.

Now, at that time, most fathers discouraged their daughters from becoming anything more than elegant and obedient wives.

But not Jane's father.

He made arrangements for his girls to have their own study.

It had blue wallpaper and blue striped curtains and chocolate-brown carpet.

It was quiet.

It was perfect.

Jane wrote and wrote in her new study, *indulging her imagination in every possible flight.*

Jane loved poking fun at the fluff, but she wanted to do more.
She started to dream about writing stories that mattered to her.
They would come from her own voice—a style that was uniquely hers.
Jane's writing was clever . . . but it wasn't yet her own.
Something was missing.

In search of her voice, Jane began to carefully observe everyone around her. She noticed details that others missed.

How her neighbor Mrs. Powlett was silly, cross, and extravagant.

How her brother James cut up his turkey with great perseverance.

How her glamorous cousin, the comtesse, enchanted everyone she met.

She noticed how small decisions could change someone's life in big ways.
And how people often said one thing while meaning something completely different.
It was *her* world.
And it was fascinating.

Jane's father saved up to buy her fancy pens and expensive blank books. To encourage her work, he gave her a portable mahogany writing desk. Jane had never felt so happy and loved.

Hidden away from the noise of the world, Jane delighted in sitting and thinking at her desk.

She started writing clever stories about her own world.

Three or four families in a country village is the very thing to work on, she thought.

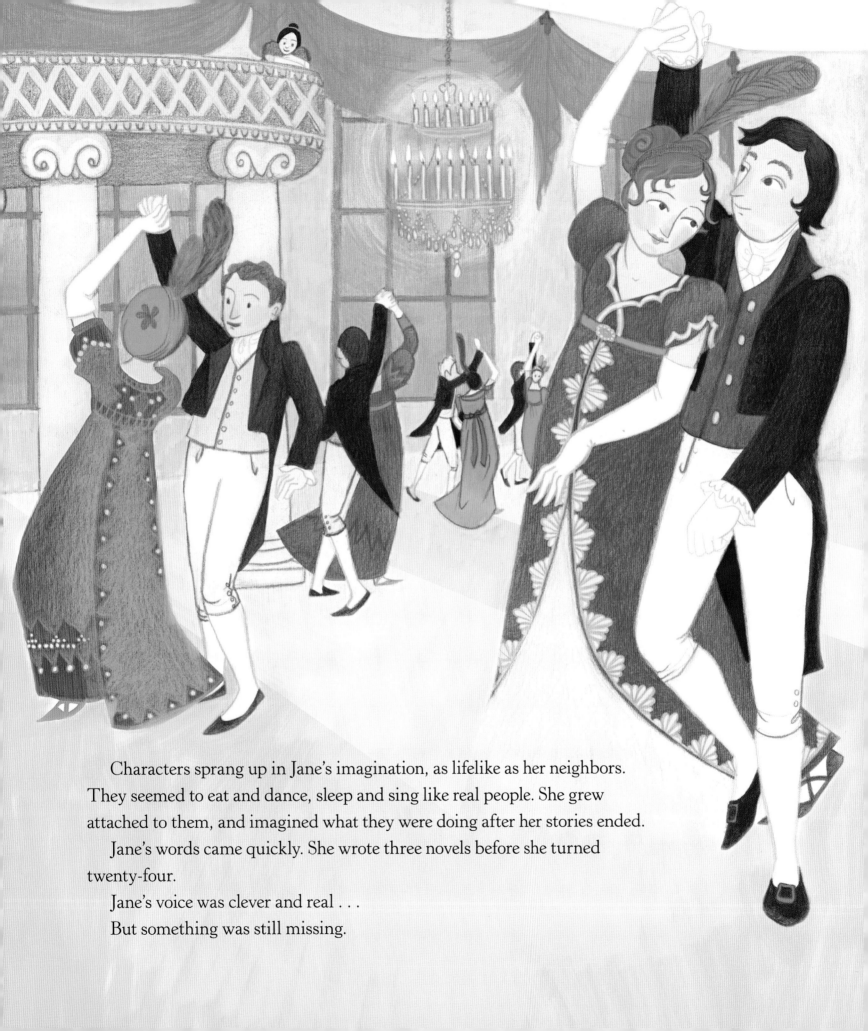

Characters sprang up in Jane's imagination, as lifelike as her neighbors. They seemed to eat and dance, sleep and sing like real people. She grew attached to them, and imagined what they were doing after her stories ended.

Jane's words came quickly. She wrote three novels before she turned twenty-four.

Jane's voice was clever and real . . .

But something was still missing.

In time, Jane's brothers grew up and left home. Her father
stopped teaching. The house grew strangely quiet. Money was tight.

Jane's parents decided to move. Jane and Cassandra would live with them in the
town of Bath, in a much smaller house. They would have to sell most of their things.

Cassandra was away when Jane's father announced the news. Anguished letters
flew between the sisters. They would be torn from their cherished friends and comical
neighbors, their fields of flowers and strawberry beds, their rambling house with its rooms
full of words and all their childhood memories.

Jane watched in disbelief as the books were sold from her father's library and the
blue striped curtains removed from her study.

Jane wondered *when she would cease to regret her loss and learn to feel a home elsewhere.*

When they arrived at their new home, Jane tucked her
writing desk in a corner.

As the days turned into weeks and months, Jane *persisted
in a very determined, though very silent, disinclination for Bath.*

Her words slowed to a trickle.

A year passed.

Then another.

And another.

And another.

Her desk just sat there.

Life became *a quick succession of busy nothings.*

Then, Jane's father died.
No words came.

Jane and her mother and sister struggled to make ends meet. They moved into a cheap apartment on a noisy, dirty street, next to a hatmaker's shop and a fire insurance office. Smoke choked the air.

Then they lived uneasily in her brother Frank's house, in a navy dock town with unsurpassably stinky streets, filled with rough men and violence.

The weight of Jane's losses threatened to drown her.

The countryside. Her childhood home, with its rooms full of words.

Her young, energetic brothers. Life without financial worries. Her friends and neighbors.

Her beloved father.

Four more gray years passed, and still Jane did not write.

Jane's brother Edward couldn't bear to see his family suffer. He gave them a little cottage in the countryside, near where Jane had grown up.

Jane's life was like it had been before, but sadder and lonelier.

Jane looked out at the landscape she had loved as a child. She remembered the girl who had imagined writing stories that only she could write. She remembered the father who believed in her. She found her way through the sadness and loneliness.

She set up her desk.
She took up her pen and started to write.
Slowly, the words came.
One word, then another.

Jane's voice was clever, as it had been in her childhood.
It was still filled with real people.
But grief and loss had added something new.
Jane's voice was wise.

Jane's characters were even more lifelike than before. Readers now saw the world through the eyes of complicated women—like the high-spirited Emma Woodhouse—and learned how hurtful snobbery could be. The bright Anne Elliot struggled to reclaim her life after following some very bad advice. The spunky Elizabeth Bennet showed up after being abandoned for ten years. Jane was finally able to finish her story.

Jane *knew where she had been—she recollected what she had seen.*
She made art out of the world around her.

It was what she knew best.

Jane's words came faster and faster.

She revised the novels she had written in her childhood home and
wrote three more.

Jane wrote the world of her sister and brothers, her father, her
rambling house. She wrote heartbreak and sadness, happiness and hope.

The clever, real, and wise were all mixed together in a way that was
completely new.

People rushed out to buy Jane's books.

They were so popular that the future king of England, George IV, read and loved
all of them. In fact, his librarian, Dr. James Stanier Clarke, asked her to write one of
those sticky-sweet love stories that she just couldn't stand . . . without any clever parts.

Jane flatly declined Dr. Clarke's request. She wrote in a letter:

I could not sit seriously down to write a serious Romance under any other motive than to save my life. . . . No, I must keep to my own style & go on in my own way.

And finally, she knew . . .

PRIDE
AND
PREJUDICE:
A NOVEL.
IN THREE VOLUMES.

SENSE
AND
SENSIBILITY:
A NOVEL.
IN THREE VOLUMES
BY A LADY.

Jane had found her voice.

Quotations

Jane Austen's work is filled with spirited and highly quotable prose,
some of which was incorporated into this book to tell Jane's own story.

*"For she had a lively, playful disposition,
which delighted in anything ridiculous."*

—Description of Elizabeth Bennet in *Pride and Prejudice*

"Know your own happiness."

—Mrs. Dashwood to Edward Ferrars
in *Sense and Sensibility*

*"Indulge your imagination in
every possible flight."*

—Elizabeth Bennet in a letter to Mrs. Gardiner about her
relationship with Mr. Darcy in *Pride and Prejudice*

*"Three or four families in a country village
is the very thing to work on."*

—Letter from Jane Austen
advising her niece Anna on her writing

*"When shall I cease to regret you!—when
learn to feel a home elsewhere?"*

—Marianne Dashwood on being forced to leave
her home, Norland Park, in *Sense and Sensibility*

*"She persisted in a very determined, though
very silent, disinclination for Bath."*

—Description of Anne Elliot on arriving in Bath in *Persuasion*

"It was a quick succession of busy nothings."

—Description of one of Fanny Price's
evenings in *Mansfield Park*

"We will know *where we have gone—we
will* recollect *what we have seen."*

—Elizabeth Bennet to Mrs. Gardiner in *Pride and Prejudice*

*"I could not sit seriously down to write a
serious Romance under any other motive than to
save my life, & if it were indispensable for me to keep
it up & never relax into laughing at myself or other
people, I am sure I should be hung before finishing the
first Chapter. No, I must keep to my own
style & go on in my own way."*

—Letter from Jane to the prince regent George IV's librarian,
James Stanier Clarke

About Jane Austen

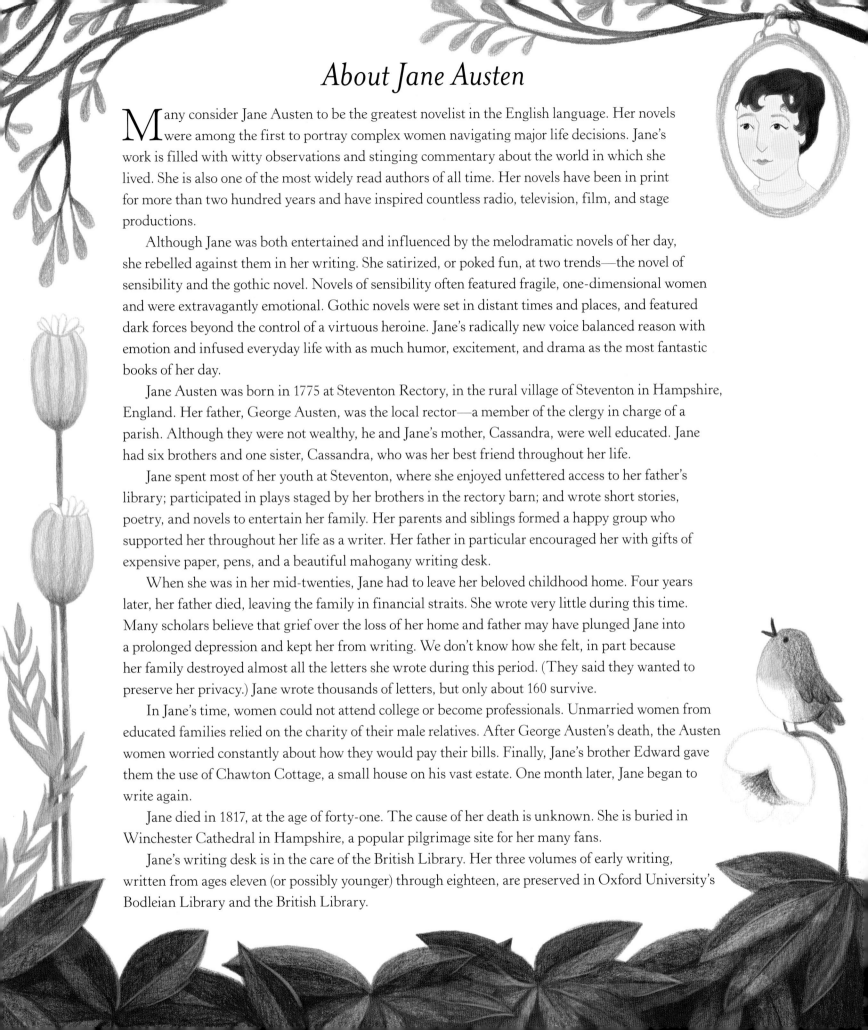

Many consider Jane Austen to be the greatest novelist in the English language. Her novels were among the first to portray complex women navigating major life decisions. Jane's work is filled with witty observations and stinging commentary about the world in which she lived. She is also one of the most widely read authors of all time. Her novels have been in print for more than two hundred years and have inspired countless radio, television, film, and stage productions.

Although Jane was both entertained and influenced by the melodramatic novels of her day, she rebelled against them in her writing. She satirized, or poked fun, at two trends—the novel of sensibility and the gothic novel. Novels of sensibility often featured fragile, one-dimensional women and were extravagantly emotional. Gothic novels were set in distant times and places, and featured dark forces beyond the control of a virtuous heroine. Jane's radically new voice balanced reason with emotion and infused everyday life with as much humor, excitement, and drama as the most fantastic books of her day.

Jane Austen was born in 1775 at Steventon Rectory, in the rural village of Steventon in Hampshire, England. Her father, George Austen, was the local rector—a member of the clergy in charge of a parish. Although they were not wealthy, he and Jane's mother, Cassandra, were well educated. Jane had six brothers and one sister, Cassandra, who was her best friend throughout her life.

Jane spent most of her youth at Steventon, where she enjoyed unfettered access to her father's library; participated in plays staged by her brothers in the rectory barn; and wrote short stories, poetry, and novels to entertain her family. Her parents and siblings formed a happy group who supported her throughout her life as a writer. Her father in particular encouraged her with gifts of expensive paper, pens, and a beautiful mahogany writing desk.

When she was in her mid-twenties, Jane had to leave her beloved childhood home. Four years later, her father died, leaving the family in financial straits. She wrote very little during this time. Many scholars believe that grief over the loss of her home and father may have plunged Jane into a prolonged depression and kept her from writing. We don't know how she felt, in part because her family destroyed almost all the letters she wrote during this period. (They said they wanted to preserve her privacy.) Jane wrote thousands of letters, but only about 160 survive.

In Jane's time, women could not attend college or become professionals. Unmarried women from educated families relied on the charity of their male relatives. After George Austen's death, the Austen women worried constantly about how they would pay their bills. Finally, Jane's brother Edward gave them the use of Chawton Cottage, a small house on his vast estate. One month later, Jane began to write again.

Jane died in 1817, at the age of forty-one. The cause of her death is unknown. She is buried in Winchester Cathedral in Hampshire, a popular pilgrimage site for her many fans.

Jane's writing desk is in the care of the British Library. Her three volumes of early writing, written from ages eleven (or possibly younger) through eighteen, are preserved in Oxford University's Bodleian Library and the British Library.

A Note from the Author

It is a truth universally acknowledged that a girl with an astonishing appetite for books must grow up to have a great many literary heroines. My particular affection for Jane Austen began when, as a young woman, I had the good fortune to study for a year as an associate member of Keble College at the University of Oxford. It was there that I began to appreciate Jane's spirited and complex characters, her wit, and her passion for *moderation*. Moderation is an unglamorous word and one rarely associated with novelists. Jane pokes as much fun at her vain and greedy characters as her romantic and impractical ones, always coming out on the side of moderation. Her heroines find happiness only when they have become more balanced people. This is one of the countless reasons I love Jane and why I decided to write a book about her for my own daughters, and other children, to read.

As I dove into my research, I fell head over heels for the Austens and even more deeply in love with Jane. Here was a rebellious girl whose outrageous writing was encouraged by her family. She lived in a magical home overflowing with boisterous boys, creativity, and music—where language was celebrated and revered. While the world of Regency England would be unrecognizable to children today, Jane's story—both its highs and its lows—is incredibly relatable.

So many of our narratives about women in history revolve around them being the first to do one thing or another. In this book, I wanted to tell a different kind of story—one centered on Jane's genius. Where did it come from? And more broadly, how do artists learn and grow over time? I wanted children to see that genius is the product of experimentation, persistence, and life's hard-won battles. And, as Virginia Woolf so beautifully argued a century later, genius must also have time, and—quite literally—space, to flourish. Indeed, without Chawton Cottage, the entire history of English literature might have looked completely different.

In the end, I hope Jane's story gives young readers insight into how to nurture their own talents—whatever they may be—to greatness.

Jane Austen's Novels

Sense and Sensibility (1811) • *Pride and Prejudice* (1813) • *Mansfield Park* (1814) • *Emma* (1815)
Northanger Abbey (1817, posthumous) • *Persuasion* (1817, posthumous) • *Lady Susan* (1871, posthumous)

Jane Austen Resources for Young Readers

Learn more about Jane, see the locations featured in this book, and watch her stories come to life:

Watch a documentary about how Jane Austen was influenced by where she lived: *Jane Austen: Behind Closed Doors*, BBC.

Visit Chawton Cottage, where Jane Austen revised and wrote her novels: https://janeaustens.house/.

Visit the Jane Austen Centre and learn about Jane's time in Bath; explore Regency-era crafts, games, and costumes; and read snippets of Jane's letters: https://www.janeausten.co.uk/.

Check out Jane's real writing desk at the British Library in London: https://www.bl.uk/collection-items/jane-austens-writing-desk.

Watch one of the many film adaptations of Jane Austen's novels.

Visit jasmineastirling.com for more recommendations and resources.

A Note from the Illustrator

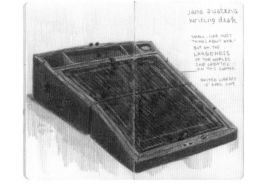

England has always been my happy place, and as an author-illustrator of historical fiction, research trips are one of the most fun parts of my job. So, to create the art for *A Most Clever Girl*, I got on a plane and took a walk in Jane's footsteps.

As I sketched, I was surprised at how small Jane's world was in every way. She hardly left the region where she was born, living in the same tiny village until she was well into her twenties. And smaller still were the spaces she occupied, sharing bedrooms with her sister, Cassandra, and owning few possessions. Her writing table, with its portable desk perched on top, would be barely large enough to hold a lamp in someone's house today. The last bedroom she and Cassandra shared in Chawton was smaller than some closets I've seen. Even Jane herself was small, as a re-creation of one of her dresses shows.

But the worlds she created! As C. S. Lewis said of the land of Narnia, Jane's "inside is bigger than [her] outside." To her, life wasn't about things, but *people*— their loves and foibles and sorrows, their growth in wisdom, or their slide into folly. People were, to Jane, an endless universe.

For the illustrations in this book, I wanted to capture the beauty of the Hampshire countryside and the bustle of the city of Bath as well as Jane's inner journey through her short and difficult life. I began by showing her youth in full color, with vibrant pinks like flowers on spring trees. She passes into a grayer time with the move to Bath, the loss of her father, and years wandering without a permanent home. Then she arrives in Chawton and finds a new maturity, which I portrayed through lush greens—but still with a bit of the young, pink cheekiness that never left her. I created these pictures with black colored pencil, and then colored them digitally, but in a way that they wouldn't lose their hand-drawn look. The book's palette comes from textile shades that were popular in Jane's time. I hope Jane becomes a friend to you through the illustrations in this book.

Selected Bibliography

Austen, Jane. *Love and Friendship: And Other Youthful Writings*. New York: Penguin, 2015.

Austen-Leigh, James Edward. *A Memoir of Jane Austen*. Edited by George Cavendish. Tunbridge Wells, UK: Solis, 2017.

Austen-Leigh, William, and Richard Arthur Austen-Leigh. *Jane Austen, Her Life and Letters: A Family Record*. London: Smith, Elder & Co., 1913.

Byrne, Paula. *The Real Jane Austen: A Life in Small Things*. New York: Harper, 2014.

Deresiewicz, William. *A Jane Austen Education: How Six Novels Taught Me About Love, Friendship, and the Things That Really Matter*. New York: Penguin, 2012.

Ross, Josephine. *Jane Austen: A Companion*. New Brunswick, NJ: Rutgers University Press, 2006.

Shields, Carol. *Jane Austen*. New York: Penguin, 2001.

Tomalin, Claire. *Jane Austen: A Life*. New York: Vintage, 1999.

Worsley, Lucy. *Jane Austen at Home: A Biography*. New York: St. Martin's, 2017.